Text : Didier Poux
Photos : Philippe Poux

BASTIDES
IN THE
MIDI REGION

Éditions
APA-POUX - ALBI
As de Coeur Collection

The creation of bastides during the Middle Ages (12th - 14th century) is a unique phenomenen in the history of urbanism.

It is situated at a time of a large increase in the French population when agricultural progress and extension of cultivated land reactivated the economic life of the country.

It was also during this period that rivalry grew between Northern and Southern France and England over Guyana. This explains the development of bastides given the complex political and economic elements.

In Languedoc, during the 20 years of the Albigensian war the king of France or his opponents created towns and bastides in a chessboard fashion.

In Guyana, the Franco-English rivalry between the Loire and the Garonne arising from the marriage of Henri Plantagenet and d'Alienor d'Aquitaine saw the arisal of English domination of several dozen bastides. The Agen region was particulary coveted.

This rivalry extended as far as the Pyrenees where bastides were created either by the king of France or of England and often by the great lords such as the Armagnacs, the Astracs the Foix or the Levis. In upper Languedoc and Quercy, the bastides created were the result of a political desire to re-inforce the French language and law.

More or less everywhere, religious orders participated in the movement especially the Cisterians and Templiers who cleared land to create new territories and bring wealth.

Most of the bastides were founded by 2 acts : a "paréage" which is an exchange of services between the co-founders of the bastide and the traditions which stated a list of rights and privileges granted to the inhabitants.

With the creation of these new towns it was necessary to attract a new population to which a certain number of economic and fiscal advantages were proposed.

There is a great diversity of Bastides which cannot always be defined according to the

same general pattern, as it has often been written. Many of them were organised in a pragmatic manner, and many others are equally characterised by their development around a pre-existing edifice such as a church or castle. Numerous bastides developed around strategic or commercial routes. Their sites are equally as varied and their plans were established in different ways according to their situations in plains or valleys or in mountainous regions. In the latter case, the bastides were built in consequence whereas in flat plain sites near rivers the town plans were influenced by the river's course. A few of the bastides were also established along bilateral axes and many were built around a central square.

Most of the bastides were fortified and have conserved parts of their ramparts and military style churches, however the fortifications were often erected after the creation of the towns. The square played and important part in the social and political life of the town. It was often surrounded by wooden framed arcades and was the centre of the town's activities. Fairs and markets were held there, it contained the public weights and measures and more often than not, a fountain.

The bastides also witnessed the creation of consulates and communal liberties and have deeply marked the history and landscape of South-western France. Their number, diversity and the quality of their architecture have today made them popular tourist centres.

Bertrand de VIVIES

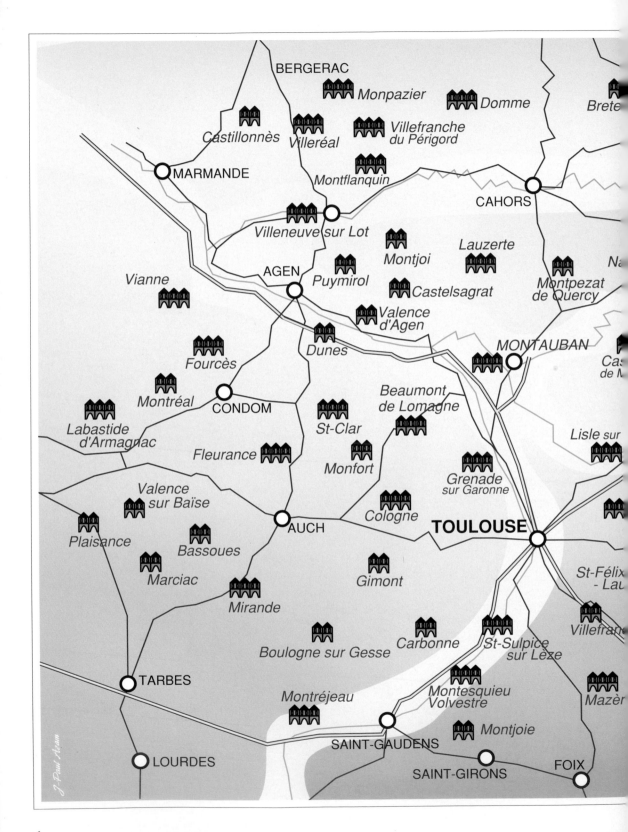

BASTIDES IN THE MIDI REGION

Cordes, the Market Place and the beautiful houses with their Gothic facades.

Neglected for many years on its hillock 110 metres high and overlooking the Cerou valley, the Medieval city of **Cordes**, miraculously preserved in picturesque surroundings reveals the treasures of its prestigious past.

The fortified city of Cordes was founded in 1222 by Count Raymond VII of Toulouse during the height of the crusade against the Albigenses. The aim was to attract the population of the area made destitute by the wars, and the city was to remain a large gathering centre for heretics during the entire 13th century. History reminds us that three inquisitors were supposedly thrown down the well on the market place (la Halle) in 1233 after having condemned people suspected of heresy. A fortified town, Cordes was protected by four or five walls, whose numerous remains can be seen today (Horloge gate, Ormeaux gate, Jane gate, etc. ...). In the 14th century, the town experienced a long period of expansion due to the flourishing leather and cloth trade. It was during this period that the rich merchants built their beautiful homes. Their Gothic facades were decorated with sculpted animal motifs which have given their name to the "House of Master Falconer" (Maison du Grand Fauconnier), the "House of the Master Squire" (Maison du Grand Ecuyer) and the "House of the Master Huntsman" (Maison du Grand Veneur). In the Midi-Languedoc, they are the finest examples of Gothic civil architecture. The plague epidemics and the religious wars were disastrous for the town's prosperity whose activities subsided for several centuries. The tourism of recent years and the restoration of the site as well as the arrival of many artists and craftsmen have brought the town back to life again. It is nowadays one of the most picturesque villages of France.

Dominating the Vere valley, the bastide of Castelnau de Montmiral.

In the heart of the Gaillac vineyards, in the Vere valley and close to the Gresigne forest, **Castelnau de Montmiral** is, like Cordes, a 13th century fortified city. It was founded by Raymond VII, Count of Toulouse. Castelnau de Montmiral has conserved Garrics' door, a part of the former city wall, its beautiful covered central square and the 16th and 17th century houses. The 15th century church features numerous works, among them a "fettered Christ", a 15th century Pieta and an exceptional 13th century reliquary cross. Today, Castelnau de Montmiral is a pleasant leisure centre.

Near the Gresigne forest which covers over 4000 hectares, you must not miss the village of **Vaour**, the old buildings of the "Commanderie des Templiers" and the village of **Penne** nestled against its formidable 11th century castle. You must also see **Bruniquel** with its castle overlooking the Aveyron river and **Puycelsi**, a fortified village and former fortress of the Gresigne forest.

Near Albi, **Castelnau de Lévis** was founded in 1235. It is a small town dominated by the ruins of its feudal castle. The huge fortress was built by the Lord of Sicard, the Count of Toulouse's lieutenant, before becoming the property of Lévis, a former companion of Simon de Montfort. Transformed into a stone quarry after the revolution, only the watch tower remains (50 metres high) overlooking the Albi plain.

In the Tarn valley, **Labastide de Lévis** was founded in 1229.

At the foot of the village, near the 15th and

Castelnau de Montmiral, Garrics' door Vestiges of the former fortified city wall.

The arcades square of Castelnau de Montmiral, an 13th century bastide.

16th century church is a beautiful pigeon-house, "Le Pradinas". It is built of stone on 8 sandstone pillars with a roof of "cow's tail" form. After Gaillac, the capital of one of the first Gaul vineyards, **Lisle sur Tarn** is a bastide built towards 1229 by Raymond VII of Toulouse after the destruction of Montagut castrum which was besieged by Simon de Montfort. The town has developed around its beautiful covered market square, one of the largest in the south-west. It is characterised by its "pountets", small bridges linking the first storeys of the old houses. The 14th century church features a fine Romanesque door and the Raymond Lafage museum exhibits the works of the famous 17th century draftsman.

Near **Rabastens**, the former base of a priory depending on the abbey of Moissac, is the bastide of **Saint-Sulpice**, the former seigneury of Gaston Phoebus, Count of Foix. It is dominated by a magnificent bell-tower wall, part of the 14th-15th century church. Also nearby are the bastides of Briatexte and **Buzet sur Tarn**.

The arcades market square of Lisle sur Tarn and the beautiful half-timbered facades of its old houses.

9

The narrow streets of Lisle sur Tarn bordering the central market square.

Mirepoix, the former consuls' residence

Mentioned as early as 1062, the town of **Mirepoix** was conquered by Simon de Montfort during the crusade against the Albigenses. It was handed over to his faithful lieutenant Guy de Levis.

In 1279, the Hers broke its banks and a dam near Puivert castle collapsed, destroying the city. After an agreement between Guy III de Lévis and the inhabitants, the city was rebuilt on the left bank of the river.

The main square is very pretty with its old half-timbered houses (13th-15th century) whose framework overhangs the arcades market. We can admire the sculpted wooden beams of the former consuls' residence which feature human and animal figures. Unfortunately, the facade was badly damaged by a fire in 1644 and a large part of the decoration was destroyed.

Begun in 1343, Mirepoix cathedral contains the largest nave of all French Gothic churches. It is characterised by its superb spire which was built during the episcopate of Philippe de Levis, from 1506 onwards.

On the sculpted wooden beams of the consuls' residence, the sculptures represent exotic animal or human figures.

The façade of the consuls' residence above the timbered arcades and wooden pillars

Mirepoix, the beautiful flowered facades of the old houses

Mazères sur l'Hers was founded in 1253 by an agreement concluded between the Count of Foix and the Abbey of Boulbonne. It became famous when the counts of Foix established their residence there. Mazères features many beautiful buildings amongst them the church, the market, the Middle Ages arcades and the residence of the counts of Foix built in the 16th century..

The bastide of **Montjoie en Couserans** was founded by Alphonse de Poitiers in 1256 on an agreement with the bishop of Couserans. It features a fortified 14th century church with a bell-tower wall and fine vestiges of its 16th century fortified wall.

BASTIDES IN HAUTE GARONNE

Aerial view of Cazères. On the banks of the Garonne, the houses around the 14th century church.

At the foot of the Pyrénées and at the confluent of the Neste and Garonne rivers, **Montréjeau** is a royal bastide built in 1272. On the banks of the Garonne, **Cazères** is a bastide founded by Alphonse de Poitiers towards 1267. It was an important stopover for the Saint-Jacques de Compostelle pilgrims and prospered due to its port. Its 14th century church contains a remarkable religious treasure.

Created in 1246 by Count Raymond VII of Toulouse, **Montesquieu** was the capital of Volvestre and has grown around its arcaded market place. Its 13th century church with its fortified facade and its 16 sided polygonal bell tower contains rich interior decoration (entombment, stone sculpture and 15th century Christ on the cross).

Like the small bastide of Salles sur Garonne, **Carbonne** was founded in 1256 by Alphonse de Poitiers at the confluent of the Garonne and the Arize rivers. **Saint Sulpice sur Lèze** was built in the heart of the forest and features superb half-timbering.

Aerial view of Saint Félix de Lauragais

Montesquieu Volvestre : 13th century fortified church

To the north of Toulouse, **Grenade** is a bastide founded in 1290 by Eustache de Beaumarchais. The small town features a Toulouse Gothic style church with a brick spire 47 metres high. Nearby, we can visit the bastides of Bouloc, Buzet sur Tarn and Montastruc.

In the Lauragais region, near the Montagne Noire, **Revel** is a royal bastide founded in 1342 by Philippe VI de Valois. On the central arcades square, the 14th century market place, reconstructed in the 19th century, has conserved its wooden framework and its belfry.

Overlooking the Lauragais plain, **Saint Félix** is mentioned in 1167, during the Great Cathar Council which was organised by the heretic church in the Languedoc region. The bastide which is a royal foundation, is characterised by its 14th century church, the collegiate building, the market-town hall and the 15th-16th century castle offering a magnificent panorama over the entire region.

The central square of Montréjeau

The market of Revel, formerly the «town house», with a prison, on the 1st floor.

Cologne : the 14th century square market place, the belfry and the bell.

Situated in the east of the Gers department, **Cologne**, formerly called Sabolène, was created on the 26th March 1284 by an agreement between Odon de Terride, the contested heir of Raimond Jourdain de l'Isle and the seneschal of Toulouse, Eustache de Beaumarchais. It is one of the finest and best conserved Gascogne bastides. On the central square surrounded by covered arches, the 14th century market place is constructed on cylindrical stone pillars with a half-timbered belfry. It contains an old 15th century grain measure. We can admire the half-timbered houses and the church with its "treasure".

Gimont was founded by Cistercian monks from Planselve who signed an agreement with the seneschal of Alphonse de Poitiers in 1265. The town is a former stopover for Saint Jacques de Compostelle pilgrims and features a 14th century church and a pretty market square which the main street runs through.

Nearby, **Mauvezin**, formerly ruled by the viscounts of Fezensaguet, features a market place built on stone pillars.

Cologne : the covered arches of the square.

The beautiful half-timbered houses, above the covered arches in Cologne

Aerial view of Fleurance, the central square and its impressive market, the 14th-16th century church.

Solomiac and **Monfort** are 13th century royal bastides.

The bastide of **Fleurance** was created during a troubled period of conflict between the local lord, Géraud de Cazaubon and the powerful Armagnac counts. These struggles were resolved by the King of France, Philippe le Hardi represented by his seneschal who concluded an agreement in 1274 with Géraud de Cazaubon. Fleurance was founded on lands belonging to the abbey of Bouillas. In the 14th century, Fleurance became one of the most important bastides of Gascogne, handed over from the King of England to the Armagnac counts, thus permanently becoming the property of the King of France in 1374.

A fire destroyed the original market building which was rebuilt in the 19th century. It now contains the large Town Hall built on 54 pillars.

Fleurance : the market finished in 1837 decorated at each corner with beautiful bronze statue-fountains representing the four seasons.

The church constructed in the late 13th century is dominated by an octagonal bell tower 40 metres high. We can admire the stained glass windows of the choir (16th century) executed by the master glazier Arnaud de Moles.

Fleurance : from the covered arches, view of the octagonal bell tower

Fourcès is characterised by its circular shape due to its development around a former feudal castle. Occupied by the English in 1289 and transformed into a bastide, it was passed over to the King of France in 1343. Its rounded central square is bordered by covered arches and old houses. The small city was surrounded by ramparts of which only a single gate - Porte de l'Horloge - remains with its bell. The town features a medieval stone bridge and a 15th century castle.

Fourcès : flowered facade with wooden panels

Fourcès : the central circular square with its beautiful stone residences.

Miélan : the market building on the square

Situated in lower Armagnac, **Miélan** was founded in 1284 by an agreement between the seneschal of the King of France, Eustache de Beaumarchais and Bernard de la Roche. The central square is bordered on two sides by covered arches over which are 16th and 17th century half-timbered houses. Over the market square with its large arcades (rebuilt in the 19th century) is the Town Hall.

Built on the left bank of the Baïse, **Mirande** the capital of Astarac was created at the same time as Pavie in 1280 to ensure protection against the English. The imposing 15th century church with its powerful buttress crossing the street gives us an idea of the importance of the town, formerly protected by strong walls. The central square has kept its arcades but the market has disappeared, replaced by a band stand. The streets are at right angles forming a chessboard of squares of 50 metres and some of them still feature half-timbered houses.

Marciac was created in 1298 by an agree-

Aerial view of Mirande : Astarac square and Notre-Dame church.

The covered arcades of Montréal du Gers

ment concluded between the Count of Pardiac, the abbot of La Case-Dieu and the seneschal of the King of France in Toulouse, Guichard de Marciac, thus the town's name. Built on forest and swamp land, it was destined to « clean up » the region which was also controlled by groups of brigands. It is oval in shape, built in five rows of five "islets" and features fine arcades. Although the market building no longer exists, it is today the venue of a renowned Jazz Festival which takes place each year during the week of the 15th August.

We owe the foundation of **Montréal du Gers** to Alphonse de Poitiers and his seneschal Guillaume de Bagnols, in 1255. It is built on a rectangular plan, formed of small islets crossed by "carreyrous" (small but rather wide streets giving access to the houses). The square is surrounded by pretty arcades communicating with the Gothic church.

The arcade square of Montréal du Gers.

Labastide d'Armagnac was founded in 1291 by an agreement between the Count of Armagnac, Bernard VI and Arnaud Guillaume de Mauvezin. A charter of customs was given to the inhabitants in 1296 by Jean de Grailly, seneschal of Edward the 1st, King of England. Situated on the left bank of the Douze, Labastide d'Armagnac was a large town and was used as a garrison by the Black Prince during the 100 years war. Constructed on an octagonal plan, the bastide is a charming town with its central square bordered by wooden framed arcades and the imposing bell tower of its 14th century church.

Situated in Upper Armagnac, **Plaisance** is one of the last bastides created in the region. We owe its foundation in 1322 to the Count of Armagnac and the abbey of La Case-Dieu. During the Middle-Ages, its development was hindered by rivalry with the neighbouring bastide of **Beaumarchès**. Created in 1288, the latter owes its name to its founder Eustache de Beaumarchais, the seneschal of Philippe le Bel in Toulouse.

The arcades of Labastide d'Armagnac and the bell tower.

Occupied by a castrum in the 11th century, **Bassoues** was built in 1295 by the Archbishops of Auch. Formerly enclosed by a fortified wall, it has conserved its powerful dungeon (43 metres high) which dominates the small town. The market occupies the entire central square and is crossed by the main street. It is a charming village with pretty half-timbered houses and the old church situated outside the walls still contains the sarcophagus of Saint Frise.

The seat of a Benedictine priory and a castrum, the town of **Saint Clar** was founded in 1289 by an act concluded between Géraud de Monlezun, the bishop of Lectoure and the King of England, Edward the 1st. It was an important bastide in the Viscounty of Lomagne and grew up first in a circular pattern around its church, then on an octagonal plan around the square and the wooden market building.

Left page : the covered arcades of Plaisance
Right page : aerial view of Saint Clar. The market with its wooden framework.

28

The arcades in Monflanquin

The house of the Black Prince (13th-14th century) in Monflanquin and the fortified bell tower

On a hill overlooking the Léde valley, **Monflanquin** is a bastide founded in 1252 by Alphonse de Poitiers and the Lord of Calviac, Guillaume Amanieu. It became English territory in 1279 and has conserved several traces of this period such as the Black Prince's house which features beautiful Gothic windows. The town is quite charming with its old sloping streets (or « carrérots »), its arcade square and Gothic church which has a fortified facade.

To the north of Monflanquin, on the edge of the Périgord region, **Villeréal** was created by an agreement between Alphonse de Poitiers, the abbey of Aurillac and the Lord of Biron. The bastide has kept its half-timbered houses, its arcades, its market over which the Town Hall is situated and its 14th century fortified church dominating the small town.

Nearby, **Castillonnès** was built on a hill overlooking the Dropt. It is an "Alphonsine" bastide founded by an agreement between the Abbey of Cadouin and the Lords of Mons. The town has conserved its square (Place des

Grailly, the seneschal of the King of England and Lord Jourdain de l'Isle, **Vianne** was a fortified town destined to protect the Agenais territories under English domination. It was constructed on the site of an old village whose small Romanesque church, Notre-Dame de Villelongue remains. Vianne has conserved numerous remains of its fortified wall with its ramparts, its town gates and its corner towers.

Cornières) and vestiges of the old 14th century ramparts.

Villeneuve sur Lot was founded in 1253 by Alphonse de Poitiers on the right bank of the Lot. In 1263 a new agreement was drawn up between the Pujols lords and the religious order of Eysses, extending the town to the left bank of the river. Considered as one of the most important bastides in the South-West, Villeneuve sur Lot was enclosed by a large fortified city wall. Pujols and Paris gates are the only remaining vestiges of the ramparts. Built of brick and stone, they were equipped with crenelations and machicolations with brown tiled roofs and a bell tower. Each side of the river features its religious edifice : Saint Etienne church on the left bank and Saint Catherine on the right bank. The latter was badly damaged by a landslide and was rebuilt in the Byzantine style. The "Pont Vieux" on the Lot, built by the English in 1289 was partly destroyed when the river broke its banks in 1599, carrying away the two arches on the right bank. The town has kept much of its charm with its arcades, its old streets and its old half-timbered houses.

An English bastide built in 1284 by Jean de

Vianne gate.

Domme : the old markets and the Governor's house

The town of **Domme** is built on "a promontory hanging between the valley and the sky" on an enormous rocky "dome" 150 metres high overlooking the Dordogne which peacefully meanders below.

Situated on an exceptional site, at the crossroads of the main regional roads, it was occupied by a feudal castle until 1280. At this time, the King of France Philippe III le Hardi built a bastide destined to affirm his power over the Périgord barons.

The city was occupied by the English during the 100 years war, then experienced numerous assaults and pillages over the years. The most dramatic was undoubtedly during the religious wars when Domme was taken by the Huguenots under the command of the famous Protestant captain Geoffroy de Vivans who contributed to the destruction of a large part of the religious edifices.

It was constructed according to the strict architectural rules for bastides with streets at right angles. Its general shape however was adapted to the surrounding land and thus took on a trapeze form.

Domme : Tours gate, vestige of the fortified walls

The old town has kept much of its charm with its pretty flower-filled streets, golden stone houses and brown-tiled roofs.

Inside the town are numerous monuments : the city wall with its fortified gates, Tours gate in which the Templiers knights were imprisoned from 1307 to 1318 (grafitti inside), del Bos gate and La Combe gate. You must also see the Town Hall, the Governor's house (15th century), the Paul Reclus museum and the 17th century market which contains the entrance to the magnificent Domme caves, formerly used as a hiding place by the town inhabitants.

From Barre lookout, there is a splendid panorama over the Dordogne valley which is even more impressive from the cliff path underneath.

Aerial view of Domme

Domme : a picturesque street and del Bos gate

Monpazier : the arcades

*Monpazier : view of the Chapter
house and the bell tower*

*Monpazier : the market building
containing old grain measures*

Monpazier was founded in 1284 by Edward the 1st, King of England and the Duke of Aquitaine, by an agreement between Jean de Grailly, seneschal of Guyenne and Pierre de Gontaud, Lord of Biron.

Similarly to Domme, Monpazier experienced troubled times. It was taken siege and pillaged by both camps during the 100 years war, then invaded by the Huguenots during the religious wars. It was also at the heart of the "croquants" revolt in 1637. Built on a four-sided plan with straight streets forming squares and rectangles, Monpazier is characterised by its regular shape and its exceptionally well conserved state.

The bastide has kept part of its ramparts and three fortified gates. The rectangular central square features arcades and "cornieres" and the market building contains old grain measures. Near the 14th and 15th century church with its 14th century stalls, the 13th century Chapter house is ornamented with beautiful geminated windows

Founded in 1261 by Alphonse de Poitiers, **Villefranche du Périgord** is a pretty bastide dominating the Lémance valley. In the heart of a large forest of oak, fir and chestnut trees, the town has kept much of its charm with its square surrounded by houses built on 13th century arcades, its market building resting on stone pillars and its old streets.

Beauregard : market building

Situated between Cahors and Rodez, **Beauregard** is a royal French bastide. It was founded by an agreement concluded in the late 13th century with the Abbey of Marcilhac, the owner of the land. Beauregard has kept its stone tiled covered market, its Town Hall and belfry, 15th and 16th century houses and its 14th century church.

Castelsagrat was created in 1269 by Alphonse de Poitiers, the Count of Toulouse. It features a pretty 13th and 14th century arcaded square and an old well. The old houses with their stone facades and the Gothic church contribute to the charm of this small bastide.

Built on a hill in a picturesque site, **Lauzerte** was occupied by a castrum in the 12th century founded by Count Raymond V of Toulouse. Transformed into a bastide in 1241 by Count Raymond VII, Lauzerte's architecture is adapted to its site. The town features a pretty square with arcades, old stone and half-timbered houses and remains of its fortified walls.

The arcades of Castelsagrat

Founded in 1144 by the Count of Toulouse Alphonse-Jourdain, the town of **Montauban** was built as a fortified bastide. It is an important link between the Quercy, Rouergue, Gascogne and Languedoc regions and was a Protestant centre in Southern France. Montauban was badly damaged during the religious wars. Built with pink bricks it is a "town of art" with many beautiful edifices : the Old Bridge (Pont Vieux) on the Tarn, Notre-Dame Cathedral, the Ingres museum and the National square with its arcades.

Founded by an agreement between Alphonse de Poitiers and the Lord of Monpezat, the bastide of Montpezat was the home of the Près family, five of whom its members were eminent church prelates. The most famous was Cardinal Pierre des Près who founded Saint Martin collegial which he consecrated in 1343.

The meridional Gothic church contains remarkable 16th century Flanders tapestries retracing the life of Saint Martin, two fine recumbent figures and a treasure whose reliquaries are 14th century.

Monpezat du Quercy, the town gate

The medieval village situated on the Limogne Causse features beautiful old homes and an arcade square.

The bastide of **Nègrepelisse** was created by an agreement between the Lord of Bruniquel and the Abbey of Moissac. It was a Protestant stronghold and was entirely destroyed during the religious wars then rebuilt after 1622.

The church bell-tower and the castle were the only buildings spared by Louis XIII's army.

Aerial view of Nègrepelisse, the square arcade place and the church.

Beaumont de Lomagne : the arcades

Founded between 1274 and 1278, **Beaumont de Lomagne** is a large bastide of pink bricks with a market building, Notre-Dame church with its imposing Toulouse style spire, its 17th and 19th century mansions and its old half-timbered houses.

The capital of white garlic cultivation and a «gastronomic» town, Beaumont de Lomagne is also a well-known equestrian centre.

Beaumont de Lomagne : beautiful half-timbered facade

General view of Najac village dominated by its castle

A picturesque old street in Najac

At the foot of its powerful fortress, the village of **Najac** was built along the entire length of a hill around which the Aveyron river flows. Of very old origin, the castle was rebuilt towards 1100 by Raimond de Saint Gilles, the son of Count Raymond IV of Toulouse and became the capital of western Rouergue. After the crusade against the Albigensians in 1252, the present fort was built dominated by its powerful cylindrical dungeon 40 metres high.

The village stretches out along both sides of the main street. Divided into different sections, the town features pretty houses, among them the arcade buildings on Faubourg square. Walking through the picturesque streets we can admire Consuls' fountain built in 1344, the Gothic church and the bridge over the Aveyron river.

At Najac, the wooden-framed arcades built on stone pillars.

Aerial view of Sauveterre de Rouergue
The fine central square with its arcades.

On the Segala plateau, **Sauveterre de Rouergue** was founded in 1281 for the King of France, by Guillaume de Maçon, the seneschal of Rouergue. The bastide was constructed on a rectangular plan with four main streets crossing each other to form eight «islets». It is characterised by its vast square of 50 by 60 metres surrounded by 15th and 17th century houses built on arcades with Gothic vaulting. Some of the buildings feature beautiful interior courtyards

Night view of the bridge of Villefranche de Rouergue.

(such as the Town Hall) and have cellar entrances beneath the arcades.

To be seen are the 14th century Gothic church and Unal house, one of the oldest of Sauveterre. Very little remains of the fortified town wall which has been transformed into a walking path.

At the confluent of the Aveyron and Alzou rivers, on the border between Rouergue and Quercy, at the cross-roads of the main Roman roads and finally on the Saint Jacques de Compostelle pilgrim route, **Villefranche de Rouergue** was and still remains an important commercial centre.

Created in 1252 by Alphonse de Poitiers on an agreement with the Bishop of Rodez, the town expanded rapidly around Notre-Dame collegial, a remarkable example of Gothic Languedoc architecture. The town was divided into four quarters or «gaches». To the North, Chapitre and Puech were close to the square and the collegial and to the South, Gua and La Fontaine which has kept its old public fountain «le Grif-

Villefranche de Rouergue square

foul», dating back to 1336.

Consuls' bridge, built in 1298, linked the town to the left bank of the Aveyron river where large fairs were held. Villefranche de Rouergue has kept many of its fine buildings such as the 18th century private mansion which houses Urbain Cabrol museum as well as religious edifices such as the 17th century Black Penitents chapel and the 15th century Saint-Sauveur charterhouse.

Villeneuve d'Aveyron was founded in the 11th century by the Bishop of Rodez around a monastery attached to the Abbey of Moissac. The bastide was created in 1230 by Raymond VII of Toulouse, then enlarged by Alphonse de Poitiers. The first church was built at the beginning of the 12th century on a model of Saint-Sepulchre in Jerusalem. It was then modified in the 14th century with the addition of a Gothic choir and nave. On the central square we can see old 13th and 15th century buildings with fine transom windows. Remaining from the fortified city wall are Soubirane or High gate formerly used as a prison and Cardaillac or Savi-

Villefranche de Rouergue square

GUIDES ALREADY PUBLISHED IN THE COLLECTION

Printed in the E.U